HORIZONS

HORIZONS

A Day With A
STONECUTTER

A Day With A
Stonecutter

by Régine Pernoud

Illustrations by Giorgio Bacchin
Translated by Dominique Clift

Runestone Press/Minneapolis
A Division of the Lerner Publishing Group

All words that appear in **bold** are explained in the
glossary that starts on page 43.

This edition first published in the United States in 1997 by Runestone Press.

Runestone Press, c/o The Lerner Publishing Group
241 First Avenue North, Minneapolis, MN 55401 U.S.A.

Photos on pp. 8, 9, 12, 13, 14 are used courtesy of Zodiaque.

Library of Congress Cataloging-in-Publication Data

Pernoud, Régine.
[Tagliatore de pietre. English]
A stonecutter / by Régine Pernoud ; illustrated by Giorgio
Bacchin. — 1st American ed.
p.   cm. — (A day with—)
Includes index, bibliography.
Summary: Describes, both factually and fictionally, the life of
a stonecutter in medieval Europe.
ISBN 0-8225-1913-5 (lib. bdg. : alk. paper)
1. Stone carving—Europe—Juvenile literature. 2. Sculpture,
Medieval—Juvenile literature. 3. Church decoration and ornament
—Europe—Juvenile literature. 4. Stonecutters—Europe—Juvenile
literature. [1. Stonecutters—Europe. 2. Stone carving—Europe.
3. Stone carvers—Europe. 4. Church buildings—Europe.]
I. Bacchin, Giorgio, ill. II. Title. III. Series.
NB170.P4713 1997
731.4'63'0940902—dc20   96-9519

Manufactured in the United States of America
1 2 3 4 5 6 - JR - 02 01 00 99 98 97

CONTENTS

INTRODUCTION

Middle Ages and *medieval* are terms that refer to a period in European history. This period, which lasted from roughly A.D. 500 to A.D. 1500, is sandwiched between the Roman Empire and the **Renaissance,** or rebirth of interest in classical Greece and Rome. The ideas that took root during the Renaissance mark the beginning of the modern era of Europe's history.

During the Middle Ages, the lives of the people of Europe were centered around two important factors—the power of the **Roman Catholic Church** and the power of the **landowners.** These two factors shaped European society.

The Catholic Church, in addition to taking care of religious matters, offered opportunities for education, fostered the arts (such as music and sculpture), and paid for massive building projects. People at every level of medieval life held strongly to Catholic beliefs, and the decorations on churches were symbols of this faith and devotion.

The landowners—usually noble lords who lived in castles—held power under a governing system known as **feudalism.** Although a lord might owe loyalty to a king, within his own territory, the lord managed agriculture, trade, and industry. He collected taxes, demanded military service, and made judicial decisions.

Most ordinary people, known as **peasants,** lived and worked on the lord's land and had few rights. They tilled his soil, cut his wood, repaired his buildings—in short, they did whatever the lord asked of them. In return, the lord used his knights to provide peace and security.

Some common folk, mainly merchants and **artisans,** were residents of towns. By about the eleventh century—the beginning of the **High Middle Ages**—Europe had many towns and several large cities. The first towns had been set up near castles, but as local trade grew, towns also developed along rivers and other commercial routes. Peasants began to leave rural areas to find jobs in towns. Craftworkers, merchants, food vendors, and innkeepers made up the towns' populations. Some peasants farmed their own land outside the towns and provided the townspeople with food.

This story of a medieval stonecutter takes place during the High Middle Ages in a region of northwestern France called Normandy. Stonecutters were respected artisans, and the best ones were chosen to work on large impressive structures such as **cathedrals** and **abbeys.** Many of their handcarved artworks—including statues, columns, and other decorations—have survived to the present day.

Series Editors

Part One

The World of a Medieval Stonecutter

This imposing group of tenth-century sculptures (above) decorates the tympanum above the western portal of the Church of St. Foy at Conques in south central France.

Most medieval churches are elaborate structures that stand out for their massiveness and intricate artistry. Common elements include **portals,** or main doorways, where carved statues and sculptures decorate the **tympanum** (the semicircular space above the doorway). More sculptures adorn the **capital,** the name given to the head of a column. A capital often decorated the place where the arched ceiling of the church met the straight line of a column.

These various types of stone-carved images made the church's architecture come alive. But what about the superb artists who carved them? Who were they?

(Above) *After stone had been cut from a **quarry** (open pit) and squared into a block, medieval stonecutters shaped it into a sculpture using mallet and chisel.*

*The town of Vézelay in central France contains an old church that was once part of an abbey (a place where monks live that is run by an abbot). One of the church's carved capitals (below far left) is shown by itself and then (below center) in its role as an architectural link between the vertical column and the arch. Finally the capital (below right) is seen as part of the church's great **nave** (aisle).*

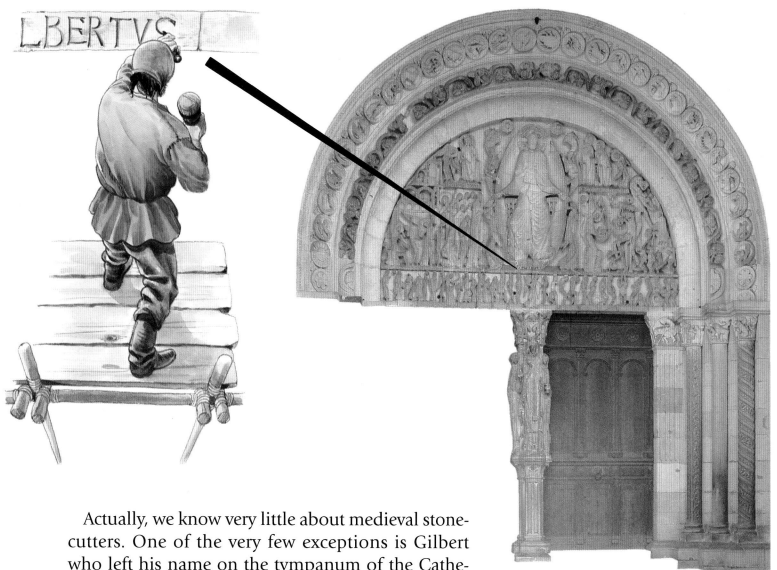

Actually, we know very little about medieval stonecutters. One of the very few exceptions is Gilbert who left his name on the tympanum of the Cathedral of St. Lazare at Autun in east central France. Just beneath the feet of a statue of Jesus, there's a small Latin inscription that reads, *Gislebertus Hoc Fecit* (Gilbert made this).

Obviously, Gilbert thought his name should be remembered, not only in the eleventh century—when he was working—but later on, too. His distinctive style of stonecutting also appears on four capitals in the same church. But Gilbert's is an unusual case. We know nothing about the vast majority of sculptors of that time.

In the above illustration, Gilbert chisels his name in stone. An arrow points to the spot on the portal where his name appears.

A stained-glass window at the Cathedral of Beauvais in northern France shows that the mason's work involved strenuous manual labor.

Records of life in the Middle Ages suggest that sculptors of stone, who were also called masons, didn't have much special training. The stonecutters who used fine tools to carve stone for buildings were not seen to be different from the workers who extracted stone slabs from quarries or who cut the slabs into transportable blocks.

In later centuries, the quarrier was a manual laborer, and the sculptor studied in a school of fine arts. In the Middle Ages, the word *artist* was not used. All those who worked with stone were artisans, because they had a craft. It was only during the six-

*Illustrations based on a book from the twelfth century depict medieval building techniques used in the construction of cathedrals. The stone, after being squared in the quarry, was hauled by cart to the construction site, where laborers unloaded the heavy blocks. The stonecutters shaped the various pieces before setting them in place. The mason on the far right is using a **plumb line** (a cord with a weight at the end) to make sure the walls are vertical.*

A drawing in a fifteenth-century book was the basis for this illustration of cathedral building in France. Notice once again the plumb line and how stonecutters reshaped the stones and prepared the cement mixture next to the actual walls.

teenth century, at the time of the Renaissance, that those who worked at a craft were distinguished from those who had acquired an education based on the ancient arts of Greece and Rome. Only then was the sculptor given higher status than the quarrier.

These images depict different types of medieval wall construction. Masons used rough stones of irregular shapes (top), as well as rectangular blocks laid with dry mortar (middle). Some walls consisted of continuous layers, called courses (bottom).

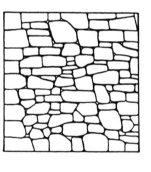
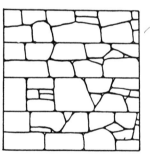
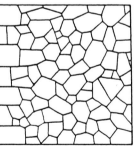
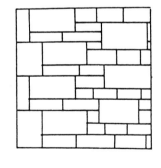
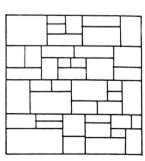
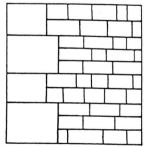

Another stained-glass window at Beauvais shows stonecutters checking their work with a plumb line.

By the twelfth century, the stages of a stonecutter's career were following the same broad outline. A stonecutter usually started out squaring blocks of stone in a quarry. The young artisan then teamed up with a more experienced **master-mason** to learn how to do the preliminary work on a sculpture. After years of training, the stonecutter started carving actual images out of stone.

This illustration depicts the layout of the Abbey of St. George. The church dates from the first half of the twelfth century, while the building to its left and the cloister, where most of the events in the stonecutter's story take place, are from the second half of the same century.

As a sign of their religious office, the abbots of St. George at Boscherville, a town near the city of Rouen in Normandy, carried this carved wooden staff (top). The piece is on display at the Museum of Rouen. The museum also holds the sculptured capital (above) featured in the stonecutter's story. Originally from the **cloister** *(covered walkway) of the Abbey of St. George, the four-sided capital shows a group of musicians.*

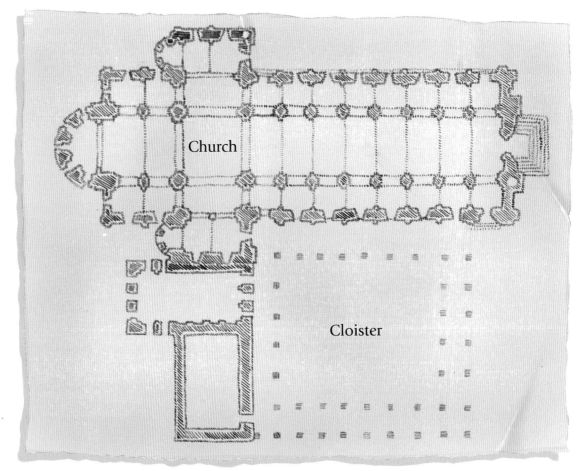

Church

Cloister

Yves, the stonecutter in the following story, is working on a capital for the Abbey of St. George in Boscherville. An abbey church was part of a monastery, a well-ordered, largely self-sufficient community where monks lived and worked. In addition to a church, the monastery had many other buildings, including a **chapter house,** monks' quarters, guest houses, kitchens, an infirmary (hospital), a brewhouse, and stables. Abbeys also managed their own farmland and livestock.

The abbey church still stands in Boscherville, although the adjacent buildings were added in later centuries.

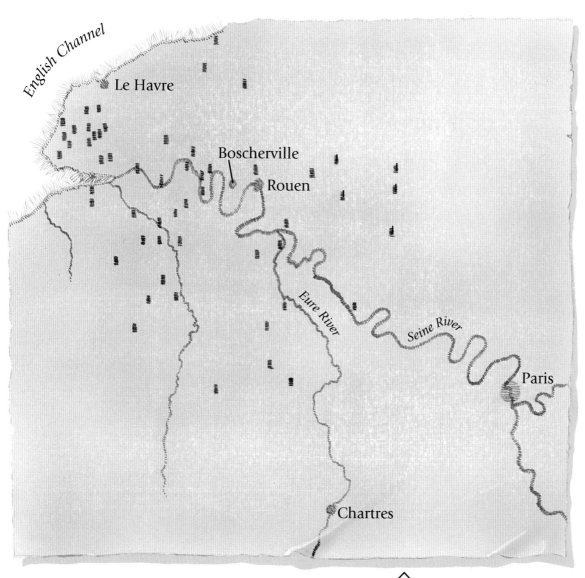

This map pinpoints the many sites of medieval cathedrals and abbeys in northwestern France, many of which were built along waterways such as the Seine and Eure Rivers. From its beginning in eastern France, the Seine River flows through the capital city of Paris to the port of Le Havre, where the waterway empties into the English Channel. The river's course takes it through Rouen and close to Boscherville. The Eure goes through Chartres, a cathedral city in north central France, before joining up with the Seine.

THE ROYAL PORTAL
OF THE CATHEDRAL OF CHARTRES

Few people in the Middle Ages, except members of the clergy and the nobility, could read or afford to own books. The imagery on and within cathedrals such as Chartres was a form of religious instruction—a visual summary of the Bible and the ideals of the Christian faith—for uneducated common people.

Fire destroyed the first cathedral of Chartres in 1134. During the rebuilding that followed the disaster, stonecutters added a huge, three-part portal that survived a second fire in 1194. The Royal Portal, therefore, dates from the mid-1100s, while the rest of the church was built at a later time.

The main scene of the central tympanum depicts the Second Coming of Christ—the arrival of Christ as judge of humankind on the final Judgment Day. Surrounding Christ are emblems that symbolize Matthew, Mark, Luke, and John, the four apostles who wrote the Gospels. The north portal, left of the center doorway, shows Christ being brought to heaven by two angels. The right or south portal features the Virgin Mary holding the Christ child between two angels.

The **lintel**—the horizontal stone beam beneath the tympanum—contains more sculptured scenes, including the twelve apostles *(center)*, angels telling the apostles to convert the nations to Christianity *(left)*, and events in the life of the Virgin Mary *(right)*.

On the sides of the three doors are carved columns that represent the kings and queens of Judah—those who, according to the Old Testament, waited for the coming of Christ. Each column has a sculpted character in a rigid pose that enhances the sculpture's architectural function as a part of the door frame. One of these columns depicts the Queen of Sheba *(left)*. To make such a column, the medieval stonecutter chipped and chiseled on the block as it lay horizontally on the ground. After the piece was finished, it was pulled upright and brought to its proper place in the portal.

Many medieval stonecutters were **itinerant**—that is, they traveled from place to place, offering their skilled services to whomever would hire them. Unlike woodworkers, who could make a living doing small-scale repairs, masons were usually in the employ of institutions—cathedrals and monasteries, for example—that funded large-scale buildings. These massive projects often required the hiring of a large number of masons at one time, and many would be brought in from long distances. But when the employers' money ran out, the stonecutters would move on to the next job.

When traveling, sculptors carried the tools of their trade in a large pouch.

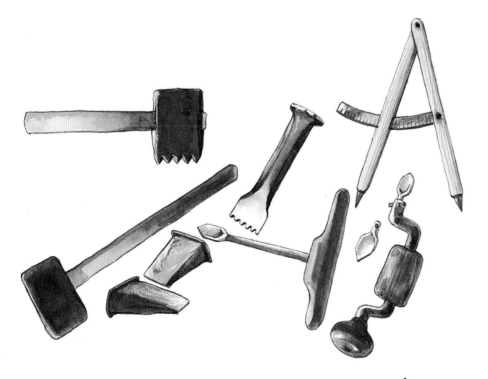

The stonecutter's tools included (clockwise from left) a toothed mallet, a chisel with a toothed blade, a compass, braces, wedges, and a flat mallet.

Yves Duclair, the fictional character in the story that follows, is a composite person whose personal traits and professional skills were drawn from a variety of historical sources.

The capital with its group of musicians is real and was part of the Abbey of St. George at Boscherville. The actual stonecutter who made the piece also worked on the Royal Portal of the cathedral at Chartres.

Because Yves is working at an abbey, he is subject to its daily routine, which includes a variety of religious services throughout the day. Lauds is a sung service that takes place just before dawn.

The Abbey of St. George is located in Normandy, a historical region of northwestern France that was the domain of the powerful dukes of Normandy. After the fall of the Roman Empire, the area was frequently invaded. By the early tenth century, Rollo, a descendant of invaders called Northmen (from which Normandy comes), had gained enough power to be named the first duke of Normandy by the king of France.

So imagine a day with a stonecutter, who has kept faith with his craft and who is dedicated to his work. . . .

PART TWO

A Day with Yves, a Twelfth-Century Stonecutter

Already at work, Yves? It's still dark. I almost tripped over that stone!"

"It's more than a stone," Yves replied to his coworker. "It's a capital for the cloister. Just a few more days of work. I'm eager to finish, so I came before dawn."

You can't work in the dark!" his friend exclaimed.

"Well," Yves said, "I figured out where to put the fiddler and the dancing woman."

"A dancer in a cloister? Are you carving the story of wicked Salome at an abbey?"

"Biblical Salome? Who asked for the head of John the Baptist? No, no," Yves said. "But I think my band of music-makers would welcome a dancer, and I have just the right place for her."

"Tell me more about your musicians after Lauds."

Guided by the sound of the choir, the two stonecutters made their way to the chapel where the monks were singing. There was no light inside except for two oil lamps, one next to the abbot and the other next to the choir leader. Little by little, as the monks sang, the chapel windows brightened. Day seeped into the chapel as first one, then another wavering ray of sunshine lit up the east side altar.

HORIZONS

21

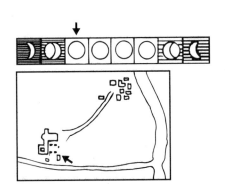

By the time the service had ended, sun flooded the chapel and the cluttered courtyard of the cloister where six or seven stone-cutters worked.

Yves crossed over to the shed to pick up his tools. He settled down before the capital that had kept him spellbound for several weeks. He was clearly proud of his work and started chiseling away at the part of the stone that was still untouched.

Yves Duclair was a master stone-cutter. Wielding mallet and chisel on this bright July morning, he recalled earlier days when he had started out in a quarry.

It was an exceptional quarry, the one at Berchères, from which they'd taken the stones for the cathedral at Chartres. The stone was magnificent, laid out in **freestone beds** so the workers were able to cut at it freely without fear of splitting the stone. It was important not to hesitate when hammering; the stone was white and solid and gave the impression it would never break. Yves remembered his first days toiling with an older mason, wondering if he would ever grow strong enough for the stonecutter's work.

Yves's parents lived in Berchères and had seen countless cartloads of stone leave the quarry. Well cut and prepared for chiseling, the stone blocks were moved one by one onto logs and, with the help of poles, heaved onto low carts.

Slow, heavy-footed oxen hauled the stone from Berchères to Chartres, about ten miles away. Once on the site of the future cathedral, each stone seemed to find its own place naturally. The solid foundation walls rose layer by layer. There was no need for cement, because after the stone sank into place it would stay there until Judgment Day.

After a while, young Yves was no longer content with quarrying and squaring the stone. One afternoon, he was watching the gestures of a stonecutter working on the Royal Portal. The stonecutter had asked him to start the preliminary work on a base for a statue. Yves found great pleasure in rounding it, always with mallet and chisel, and finally in polishing it. The skill Yves showed with his hands impressed the master-mason, who asked Yves to prepare the outline of the statue he was planning.

Yves would remember the piece all his life—it was the statue of the Queen of Sheba. With the help of a sketch, the young stonecutter chipped and chiseled and polished.

From then on, Yves worked at the Royal Portal. He was done with the dust and deafening noise of the quarry. He was free and out in the open air. Even when it rained, he preferred staying at the portal making a life-size statue. As a child, he'd drawn figures in the sand on the riverside. Now he was making figures out of stone and standing them on their feet. What a life!

The day came when Yves needed to find more work, and so he left Berchères and the cathedral at Chartres. He'd heard that in other parts of Normandy they were building new abbeys.

With a knapsack on his back and his tools in a pouch, Yves made his way along the Eure and Seine Rivers and finally arrived at the Abbey of St. George in Boscherville. Rumor had it that the abbott wanted to decorate the entrance of the chapter house (meeting hall) with an ornate capital. Because it would sit on top of two small columns, the capital would need to be double in width. Eager to be hired, Yves had pressed his case by promising the abbot a masterpiece.

He'd heard that the abbot was a music lover, and, after thinking it over, Yves agreed to the abbot's suggestion of carving figures of music-makers on the double capital. Yves himself quite liked music and felt very enthusiastic about the idea. And he was pleased with his new surroundings.

The abbey was on the edge of Roumare Forest, which contained the famous Wolf's Oak. This was the tree where Rollo, the first duke of Normandy, had suspended some gold bracelets. Rollo's domain was so well administered and watched— everyone also had enough to eat—that the duke found his bracelets, a year later, exactly where he'd left them.

The abbey bell tolled for lunchtime. The stonecutter's meal certainly had more flavor and variety than what was available in the monks' dining hall, where there was never any meat. Those who worked on the stones in the yard enjoyed a thick slice of mutton with crushed beans, bread, and a glass of wine.

Yves was just savoring the last of his wine when the abbey's treasurer tapped his shoulder.

ou'll have an important visitor this afternoon," the monk said. "The Lady of Tancarville is coming. She often gives money to the abbey and will be happy to see the new capital."

Feeling deeply honored, Yves rushed to clean up a bit at a natural well next to the abbey. He shook off the morning's layer of dust from his blue tunic, combed his hair, and cleaned his leather boots with tufts of grass.

He barely had time to return when he saw the lady and greeted her from afar.

Amid the stones and noise of the yard, Yves described his work.

"Here, my Lady," Yves pointed, "I want to bring many musicians together on this double capital. Here is a harpist with the instrument on his knee. Here is the carillonneur in front of his bells."

"I can almost hear them," interrupted the lady. "The *tintinnabulum*," she added, using the Latin word for the ringing of bells.

Yves was happy that she appreciated his plans. "And then you have the hurdy-gurdy," he continued. "The musician turns the wheel and plays with his fingers on the strings. The next musician plays the panpipes. He's raising the instrument to his lips. Next to him are musicians all with stringed instruments—the kithara player, the lyre player, and then the one who holds the psaltery. Finally, here is the rebec player with his bow."

"And what will you have here?" asked the lady pointing to a form that was barely sketched in stone.

"It will be a dancer, my Lady. Isn't music made for dancing?"

"These musicians are all wearing magnificent clothes. It seems we have an orchestra of princes."

"All musicians are princes, don't you agree?" cried Yves, full of emotion. "They excite us, they inspire us, they make us sing."

"But what about the dancer?" the Lady of Tancarville wondered aloud, a trace of anxiety in her voice. "She doesn't seem to have much space for her movements."

"I thought of having her move like an acrobat, her head down and one leg up in the air. This will make for a beautiful draping effect," Yves explained.

"My compliments, this double capital honors you," the lady said warmly. "It will be admired by all those who enter the chapter house. Normandy is being covered with splendid abbeys. Yet, not such a long time ago, my ancestors had a reputation for plundering the cities and the countryside. And do you know that it's the same with the **Magyars** who live east of us in Hungary. They also used to pillage everywhere. I hear that these days they are building superb structures in cities like Buda and Pest. Wouldn't you like to visit the Magyar lands?"

"Why not, my Lady? I am willing to go anywhere there are fine stones to work on!"

The Lady of Tancarville smiled and moved away with a friendly farewell gesture.

Laon

Lausanne

Paris

Boscherville

Buda
Pest

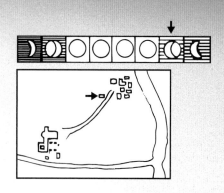

As the day faded into nightfall, Yves was filled with happiness. Not only did his noble visitor understand him, she also encouraged him. People recognized his talent. He could go anywhere and show he knew how to make stone speak.

With his love of travel, why couldn't he go to Hungary, he thought? Wherever there were churches to be built, there would be capitals to create. Even these Magyars, who used to terrify other nations, are now converting to Christianity and building cathedrals. People—particularly builders—understand one another.

He decided to obtain a few sheets of parchment on which he would sketch his most forceful figures. He would propose them to the master-masons at construction sites on his way toward the east, toward the rising sun.

The time for sleep soon arrived, and Yves made his way back to Genetay, a village near Boscherville, where he rented a room. From there he had a magnificent view of the flowing waters of the Seine. He lingered, contemplating the sunset before lying down and falling asleep with thoughts of travel. He could almost hear the musicians he had brought to life from stone. They were calling him from far away, from the direction of the rising sun.

AFTERWORD

By the late fifteenth century, changes had occurred in Europe that helped to draw the Middle Ages to a close. For example, building schemes on a massive scale became rare, so the job of the stone-cutter also changed. Sculptors drew support from royal courts and wealthy merchant families, rather than from the Roman Catholic Church.

The growth of trade that had begun in the High Middle Ages made people less dependent on agriculture for their living. As a result, the feudal system of governing became out of date. Traders and diplomats who traveled throughout Europe became exposed to and then spread new ideas, including a fascination with the ancient civilizations of Greece and Rome. This fascination developed into the Renaissance, or rebirth, of classical studies.

The Roman Catholic Church also came under fire at this time from a movement known as humanism. Rooted in the writings of ancient Greece and Rome, humanism puts great value on human beings and on their central place in nature and society. The Church, on the other hand, had long emphasized its role between God and Roman Catholics. The medieval Catholic belief—that people were sinful and should work hard to earn heaven—contrasted sharply with the humanistic view that people are good and deserve admiration. From these ideas also sprang the Reformation, a Europeanwide movement to reduce the Church's power and to change some of its laws and teachings.

Humanist ideas, which the newly invented printing press helped to spread, influenced the arts and education. The stiff, large-scale sculptures of the Middle Ages gave way to the more realistic, flowing pieces of the Renaissance. Subject matters for art and music went beyond religious themes to include mythology and contemporary events.

The ideas of humanism, including a rejection of rule by only a few wealthy families, remained popular long after the Renaissance ended. These ideas had a strong impact on the governments that were set up in France and the United States in later centuries.

Glossary

abbey: A place where monks live.

artisan: A person skilled at a certain craft.

capital: In construction, the head or crowning feature of a column. The name comes from the Latin word for head.

cathedral: A church that is the official headquarters of a bishop.

chapter house: The hall where the abbot meets with his advisers. The chapter house often looks out on the cloister.

cloister: A covered passageway enclosing a square courtyard where monks could read and walk in the open air.

feudalism: The land-based governing system that operated in Europe from the ninth to about the fifteenth centuries.

freestone bed: In quarries, a visible layer of stone of the best quality that may be cut freely without splitting.

itinerant: Traveling from place to place.

landowner: Under the feudal system, the owner of agricultural land who had power over every aspect of life on the property and made up Europe's ruling class for 400 years. Feudal landowners, in addition to managing their estates, could tax farmers, demand military service, arrange marriages, and impose judicial decisions.

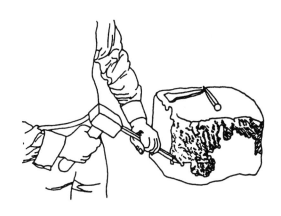

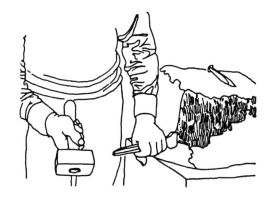

These drawings depict a stonecutter shaping a block of stone with different types of chisels, one with a pointed blade (above) *and the other with a flat blade* (below).

lintel: A horizontal beam above a doorway.

Magyar: A member of the dominant people of Hungary.

master-mason: An experienced medieval stonecutter who often hired and directed the work of other stonecutters.

Middle Ages: A period of European history that lasted from roughly A.D. 500 to A.D. 1500. The greatest achievements of the period, known as the **High Middle Ages,** came in the eleventh and twelfth centuries.

nave: The area inside a church that includes the main altar and center aisle and that is reserved for those who officiate at religious ceremonies.

peasant: A person who tills the soil on land that usually belongs to someone else.

plumb line: A cord that has a weight at one end and is used to determine if a wall or other structure is vertical.

portal: A grand or imposing doorway.

quarry: An open pit excavated to expose building stone, slate, or other material.

Renaissance: A period of European history that followed the Middle Ages and blended into the modern era.

Roman Catholic Church: A Christian religious organization that was founded in the late Roman Empire. After the empire's fall in the fifth century A.D., chaos followed. The Catholic Church became the main source of leadership, political power, and education until the feudal system evolved in the ninth century.

tympanum: The semicircular space above a portal that was often richly carved with complex groups of sculptures.

A twelfth-century capital at St. Servatius Church in Maastricht, the Netherlands, is the basis for these illustrations of medieval stonecutters.

Pronunciation Guide

Autun	oh-TU^{N}
Beauvais	boh-VAY
Berchères	behr-SHAYR
Boscherville	boh-shehr-VIH
carillonneur	kahr-uh-luh-NUHR
Chartres	SHAHRT
Eure	UHR
feudalism	FYOO-duhl-ih-zehm
Genetay	jeh-neh-TAY
itinerant	eye-TIH-nuh-rehnt
kithara	KIH-thuh-ruh
Le Havre	luh AHV
Magyar	MAAG-yahr
medieval	mee-DEE-vuhl
psaltery	SAHL-tuh-ree
Renaissance	REHN-uh-sahns
Rouen	roo-AHN
Roumare	roo-MAHR
Salome	suh-LOH-mee
Seine	SAYNE
Tancarvill	tahn-kahr-VIHY
tintinnabulum	tihn-tuh-NAA-byeh-luhm
tympanum	TIHM-puh-nuhm
Vézelay	veh-zay-LAY
Yves Duclair	EEV doo-CLAIR

Further Reading

Bracons, José. *The Key to Gothic Art.* Minneapolis: Lerner Publications, Company, 1988.

Clements, Gillian. *The Truth About Castles.* Minneapolis: Lerner Publications Company, 1988.

Fine, Joan. *I Carve Stone.* New York: Thomas Y. Crowell, 1979.

France in Pictures. Minneapolis: Lerner Publications Company, Geography Department, 1991.

Gandiol-Coppin, Brigitte. *Cathedrals: Stone Upon Stone.* Ossining, NY: Young Discovery Library, 1989.

Howarth, Sarah. *Medieval People.* Brookfield, CT: The Millbrook Press, 1992.

Howarth, Sarah. *Medieval Places.* Brookfield, CT: The Millbrook Press, 1992.

Langley, Andrew. *Medieval Life.* New York: Alfred A. Knopf, 1996.

Martell, Hazel Mary. *The Normans.* New York: New Discovery Books, 1992.

Perdrizet, Marie-Pierre. *The Cathedral Builders.* Brookfield, CT: The Millbrook Press, 1990.

Wilkinson, Philip. *Building.* New York: Alfred A. Knopf, 1995.

Index

About the
Author and the Illustrator

Régine Pernoud, an internationally known expert on life in the Middle Ages, studied at L'Ecole de Chartres and L'Ecole du Louvre before becoming curator successively of the Museum of Reims in Reims, the Museum of the History of France at the National Archives in Paris, and the Joan of Arc Center in Orléans. A resident of Paris, Ms. Pernoud is the author of more than 40 scholarly works translated into many languages.

Giorgio Bacchin, a native of Milan, Italy, studied the graphic arts in his hometown. After years of freelance graphic design, Mr. Bacchin has completely devoted himself to book illustration. His works have appeared in educational and trade publications.